COMPARING
LIGHT

COMPARING LIGHT

T C WALSHE

atmosphere press

Contents

SECTION ONE

A Lane to Damascus 3
Night's Biting.. 6
Blinding 8
Inching Towards the Sun 10
Capturing Metaphors 13
Who Knows Who 15
(Just) Remember 17
Lost on the Edge 18
Tumult 19

SECTION TWO

Feelings in Time 23
Hidden in the Wind 25
Running down the Ladder 27
Now 29
Proof in Embers 30
Swimming on Ice... 31
Bursting.. 33
Screaming in Time 34
(yes) 36
Holding Tears.. 38

SECTION THREE

Hunger at the Sun Dial.. 43
An Uncertain Wish.. 45
Blind Hope.. 49
When Angels Flew 51
Sleeping Horses 53
The Thrill of Breathing.. 56
A Sense of Timing... 58

In Wonder 60

Such Sweet Gifts 62

Was it Ever Enough 64

When Dust Settles 65

SECTION FOUR

Off 69

Longing 71

Everything is Never 73

Carried Wisdom 75

Shifting 76

The Slowness of Time 78

Holding Fire 80

Rushing 82

Asleep in Heaven 84

In Fog 86

Some Troubled Mind 88

SECTION FIVE

Lov (sic) 93

Gone 95

Melt 96

Sometimes Forgotten 97

Love Glimpsed 99

Nowhere Soon 100

Sleepwalking through a Dream 102

Screaming the Walls Down 104

Not Now 106

Blinking in the Dark 107

In Time 109

Cold Saw 110

SECTION SIX

A Kind of Choice 113

Knowing When...115

By Hurricanes 117

Something for Tomorrow 118

Old Mirrors.. 120

Treading Carefully 122

Shadow Seen...124

safe..126

A Certain Fury 127

Remembering Snow..130

SECTION SEVEN

Langley Green.. 137

In Larkspur 138

Near Cherry Lane...140

At Ifield Shops...142

The Embassy Cinema 144

Around Queen's Square 147

One Night in the Johnnie.......................................150

Chasing Stars...152

The Day When Night Arrives 153

SECTION EIGHT

The Tiredness of Sleeping 157

Where They Stood 161

Comparing Light 163

Stilts 165

This (is)...167

Some Glorious Miles...169

Nothing 171

Watching Swallows... 173

SECTION NINE

Aplomb 177

The Sadness of Knowing 179

Awake on the Avalanche 181

Setting the Seas on Fire 183

Silent Moments...186

In a Different Lift......................................187

Pure Grace...189

Burnt Sacrifices.. 190

SECTION TEN

Catching Rainbows 193

In Awe..194

An Impression..196

Beyond the Curve......................................197

Just in Whispers 198

Boys Own 199

Eclipsed.. 201

Akin..202

Landfill...203

Flirting with Wasps 204

Stirrings from the Furnace 206

SECTION ONE

When I wake on a clear day
I see mountains I once slept on.

A Lane to Damascus

Ago...

Who unleashed those monsters
that chased us
to the streams.
Gleamed banshees.
Screaming biblical taunts
from arcane sweet
dripping teeth.

Creature comforts
were never for us.
The sky so measured.
Deep in dusk.
Such a benevolent
rare beauty.
Singed within
our weathered cusp.

Such blackness.
The eternal torments.
Believe me we
were so cute.
Spinning on endless
vibrant moments.
Such boldness.
So pure and resolute.

But...

I peered into
my fractured world
that suddenly
pulled me in.
I closed my eyes.
Closed my dreams.
I trusted nothing.
Feared everything.

Alone in the lane.
Feeling exposed.
Digesting memories I
knew I shouldn't have.
The child inside me.
A hand inside.
The girl before me.
Legs astride.
No more searing screams.
Naked sighs.
Curdled lust spiralled.
Scorched night.
Reality spiked.
A graceful velvet ant bite.
Such wonder transcended
my famished light.

Those riddled times
nearly destroyed me.
And I'm not sure
why I'm here.

Trust us we'll
show you everything.

You'll never go that far
from anything
that you truly desire.
Every euphoric thought
you've longed for.
Will form the panoply
of your ravishing fire.

Night's Biting

You licked the frost from my lips.

Remember.

At Northgate shops.
Mid-December.

Two am.

Near the border with Langley Green.

The coldest night
there'd ever been.

Wrapped up.
As our
dusk's breath
crackled.

In moon's light.

All I wanted to do
was bury myself inside
your welcoming gleam.

In the park shadows
lit the fuse.
As we remained
ice-trodden.

Taking in a moment's pause.

Reflecting.

We cleared our throats
and slid alongside.

Knowing I never wanted
to grow old.
We delved deeper
into night's biting cold.

As a firestorm
glowed in winter.

We saw everything
so much brighter.

Blinding

I wasn't melting as
we met the beach.
All the shadows
had disappeared.
The pirates that
weren't lost
had vacated their
simmering post.

On that prized
gossamer cliff.
As the sea
sank from view.
You looked on.
Distant waves.
The crowd mimicked
'*a happy day*'.

In the forest of
afterthoughts.
Running around
haloed haunts.
Graceful.
Everything felt so right.
The message scrawled
'*My soaring kite*'.

In a haze of another
vivid dream.
Sun winked.
Precious joyous things.

No venture gained.
No delights unbound.
Buried deep in
the blinding sand.

Inching Towards the Sun

To leap ahead
before thinking
crisscrossed my
mind every day.

Panic consumed
all my thoughts.

At times I tried to
meet you halfway.

Trapped between
hesitancy.

Buoyancy.

I was inching
towards the sun.

Every moment
noted by everyone.

A tide sucked
by lukewarm gratitude.

Was I ever
going anywhere
to touch
moments so true.

Who knew where
we were.

Echoing around
pastures far from new.

I was staring
into thick air.

Ripped up mountains
with bare hands.

Screaming into
blank history books.

Trying to see
why I bothered at all.

All we did was
run the clock down.

And regurgitate the
same garbage again.

The urge to run
disturbed me
every day.

Watching life's
ridiculous actors.

Playing games in
their inimitable way.

Lamentable.

I'm done with
these interlopers.

In a verdant field
the boy dances in time.

Spinning in tune.
With no clear borderline.

Serene in
hypnotic gleam.

Enveloped in
a life's dimension.

As I'm inching
towards the sun.

Capturing Metaphors

Suddenly I'm gone.
A metier from another time.
The springboard arrowed fine.
To you.
Landing with aplomb.

As marinated heartbeats
in catacombs of bold feats.
Swallowing everything on view
in that mesmeric dazzle pit.

A choice to consume.
Bouncing reminders.
Never presumed.
Recognising those burnt embers.
Torn vestiges.
Dark days in September.

A dislocation.
Everything we expected.
Comparing Actifed with red wine.
Squeezing through
a portal to catch air.
Your face so
captured for all time.

Jumping beyond
chosen moments.
Finding fury in
battled atonements.
Pitched amongst

those intricacies.
Fevers kept.
The glorious endearment.

When lights stopped
us in our tracks.
Taking moments.
Standing back to reflect.
Floating amidst
the mainstream
was never our
chosen scene.

Thinking about things
I wouldn't be.
Heartfelt understandings.
All that synergy.
As shadows locked.
Minds I didn't trust.
You didn't think again.
Just floated away like dust.

Who Knows Who

When I wake on a clear day
I see mountains I once slept on.

By roundabouts nothing happened.
Castings threw me sideways.

In silence of unfeigned majesty
I grasped powders of light.

Crystal memories dappled in poise
were never answered or ever found.

I kept things close.
A shift in memory.
But I once knew you.

Staggered friends came blindside.
But who noticed me then.

Shifts of thought beyond a blur.
Dancing as I skipped in the fire.

Blinding bursts of wonder
in shadows of tender glory.

You once stood before me
in dreams of New Town splendour.

From playgrounds I found moments
that burned the thickness of time.

In darkness I captured your smile.

The last vision in a mesmeric sky.

I kept things close.
A shift in memory.
But I once knew you.

Didn't I.

(Just) Remember

I was cruising in God's slipstream
when your brakes hit my main dream.
Moments when we were once out takes.
Now run arounds for the hard acts.

On a balcony with smoking flowers.
The springboard for many adult hours.
Same time meant no firm favours.
A spare room held all the answers.

The crowd crushed the real threat.
As buried demons cured their old habits.
Simple things were never seen.
Watching the kids throw out the last guest.

While little men drank in rancid streams.
Monsters unleashed their lethal schemes.
Being kind was never like a child lock.
As everyone disappeared into God's lap.

Lost on the Edge

The triumph of seeing you eventually fly.
Presented feelings that burned inside.
The fool in me knew nothing about yesterday.
As all my joys had trenchantly arrived.

I remember running by the industrial estate.
An agony.
Holding me down further.
Insecurities beamed across a windless night.
Dripping like emerald dreams asunder.

Sitting on the kerb watching my world collide.
I scrambled along the edge.
Looking down.
Hallucinations claiming they were mine.
As the moon glowed against the silver dark.

An emerald dress kissed your silhouette.
I cried your name out in the suffocating gloom.
You turned.
Advanced toward my gestured plight.
An angel descending into my shivering room.

Tumult

Up close.
Up so fucking close.
Blood on your eyes.
Looking morose.

A conflict of interest.
Forever choked.
Vestiges of being lost.
Timely evoked.

Not simple to simply decide
whether you felt anything inside.

Actions you fiercely prescribed.
Dancing in swamps on borrowed time.

Floating above the moon's tricks.
You kept light.
The silent feat.

Bottled in that stolen fragrance.
Collecting shadows in locked frissons.

The shame of anyone believing
was there for everyone to see.

Was I asleep when you crawled by.
Reckless.
Oblivious.
Never barely alive.

A world collapsed in open sight.
Faces burned under dark light.

(No one held their breath).

Running after you
in a storm and a glare.

Quivering dogs stopped to stare.
Cynical.
They knew
why you are there.

Time ravaged by stunned fecklessness.
A life marked in trite emptiness.

SECTION TWO

Carrying lightening home was never easy.

Feelings in Time

With our sated bodies strewn
 across wet lawns.
Withering in time
as luck's remembrance.

We craned our necks.
Envied colours of the moon.
Will we ever have anything
like this again or soon.

Did we recognise
those swift encounters.
Digested days nestled in slumber.
Or held in clipped wonder.

We'll never experience now.

Whenever.

Never sure if the
mermaid held her breath.
Smiling in sequence.
Punching above her weight.

Grandstanding.
Understanding
every fractured light.
As she drowned
in Crawley's diaspora vortex.

Soft tears captured
a time of the day.
Swan songs entangled in
luminous mind games.

Sanity from brevity.
Distant daydreams.
Our lives condensed
in every film
we'd ever seen.

Hidden in the Wind

(You lit up the warmth.
Moulded splintered paths into streams.
Hope bounced around like fireworks.
Memories buried in envied chasms).

So near to morning I
didn't need to look.
Whether you were near me
or you were not.
In the mist I hurtled
into silver innocence
holding something gold.

Watching all the bonfires
in the centre of town.
Captivated.
I threw myself at them.
Their redness
caught your eye.
You're there.
As we sank together
in our fire-caught world.

The scented lino took
time to kick in.
The smoke-hued room
turned translucent in the rain.
I dipped my eyes into
your keen face.
Never knowing if you
were concerned or sublime.

But...

...looking again and you were gone.
Vanished.
Hidden in the wind.

A sacrificial lamb.
My haunting scar.
Reality emptied into
my beaten heart.
Once we were giants
breezing through town.
Second-guessing everyone
who danced in time.

I lost my innocence in
the light of your eyes.
An epiphany unfolded
in lemon breath.

In a tenebrous hall
memories faded in thin air.
At last unfurled.
Free to breathe again from
the painful nightmare.

Running down the Ladder

Carrying lightning home was never easy.
Like folding raindrops inside a full moon.

As every second was a second tamed.
I fell backwards into the fierce rain.

Leaning in.
A cold ceiling beckoned.
The lounge opened up.
Orange and blue.

My secret cocooned in a precious hue.
A room on fire with a chiselled view.

In a kitchen the ring danced in time.
Costello's debut.
You bought me for mine.

Your look.
A keenness to speak with grace.
Lost in a spark.
Drowned in emptiness.

In the crosshairs of your sharpened tongue.
Inside the cinema watching Easy Rider.

Moving beyond the dark I saw you as one.
In a frenzy.
Exploding from the ether.

Challenging nuances.
Everything so clear.

Reality bitten.
Our moment disappeared.

Now...

Into your blazing eyes sleep dust surprised.
Maddening ghosts playing inside.
A head marinating bittersweet lies.
Crushed everything I wanted and besides.

Hell bent.
Mind swept.
A life lost in my future.
Truth.
Misguided.
Shipwrecked under an ocean.

I thought you would be with me forever.
Shell shocked.
I am running down the ladder.

Now

By the benign water's edge.
Toes dipped in just for a try.
Behind him someone's about to dive.
Kids skimming stones from the other side.
And he's in her gaze so she
doesn't need to let him go.
Whatever happens in time
will always be for now.

Proof in Embers

When the penny dropped.
It always seemed to
drop into your hands.
Smoothing over every other
sequence.
Vivid moments
held tight within a glance.

Tipping every trick and
comeuppance I lay on the roof.

Would I ever see you again.

Nothing to struggle with or
to remember.
A sorry farewell
evidenced in
burning embers.

Sitting in the road
by the kerb.
An assembly
of just one boy.

Shell shocked.

Waiting for the
moment to recover.

Swimming on Ice

The shoulder to cry on
was eclipsed by the truth.

The moment he ran out
was the street cry to let loose.

In sunlight he craved darkness.
His fierce breath.

So burnt.

Blunt denials amid keen gasps.
An epiphany in glory running feet.

To the heartened belly up.
Maddening scarecrows seeking flight.
Serenely in dusks lambent moonlight.

Sipping memories from the maypole.
Was never easy or playful.

Nuisance was never a guarantee.
As shadows knelt
down pushing back extremes.

Comfort was sometimes nestling there.
Eclipsed by the presence of a cold stare.

The spark.
The maddening night out
was when he never really cared.

Staggered thought waves
silenced his lying clowns.

As time behaved differently
in his rubber band world.

Bursting

I'm carving daydreams in tree trunks.
Running through cornfields to keep up.
Known street signs never helped me.
As more time became my destiny.

I'm soaring in wanderlust.
Crafting the moon's wink from stardust.
But it sometimes nearly killed me.
The gift.
Your ethereal beauty.

Conjuring up covert defaults.
As nothing was there to see.
Losing your elevating star.
High above now.
 Arrowing in from afar.

Bittersweet days kept in ranks.
Longing to secure any vacant lots.
I was never going to lose my face.
As the sky turned slowly against.

When I sensed you near me.
Caressing the anointed fairy tree.
Forgetting about any venal street hassle.
My life.
A bursting Roman candle.

Screaming in Time

It was never her intention
to make out she was even.

The subtle cost of
being somewhere
was being truthful.
The right atmosphere.

He was always sulking off.
Into dank subways
or barren hilltops.

A simple smile.
A nice aside.
We knew all about
his cynical denials.

Ages have gone
by haven't they.
Thinking was never
gonna be easy.

Her face once a
picture to treasure.
Today so derelict.
A crushed parade.

She was sunk
deep in time.
Taking up what she
thought was mine.

So buried in
her pitied anxiety.
As it was always
meant to be.

The sweetness
in knowing all
her attributes were cloying.

As I knew it
never felt right.

The moment she
screamed that night.

(yes)

The uneventful
event of nothing
captured everything
he meant.
Remembering
those desires to go
while singing
tearful afterglows.

Spinning around
in dizziness.
Exiting before
he'd showed me.
Drawing lines to
capture cruel moments.
Saying '*yes*' to
everything I did for him.

Keeping tempers
on timed remote.
Crept into corners.
Trying to change route.
But fealty was
always subsumed.
Anchored emotions
dominated us again.

Shouting answers from
those behind us.
Made nonsense for
the real precursors.

Head scorched
by light flares.
Standing out
within my keen desires.

Pickled pink
between night sheets.
Balancing everything
in kitchen sinks.
Trying to catch
elusive burnt things.
If only signs were
what they seemed.

Running through quick sands.
Holding up a
white flag for you.
Watching me
you shouted '*yes*'.
As you sank
into the wilderness.

Holding Tears

It wasn't me who
lent you time.
It was history.
Your asinine crime.
The mixtures
bubbling high.
Results engendered
spangled minds.

A visit to
your hidden place.
Blizzard guesses.
The different face.
You lied before
that first gaze.
A wakeup call
in another haze.

In those burning times.
Ever marked
for real concerns.
Who fed the genie a
get-out clause.
Released monsters
in pristine gorse.

Did the funeral
catch you blind-sided.
Tricks mixed up.
All disconnected.
Never mind the feelings.

The lies.
All wrapped up in
razored tongue ties.

Holding your gilded tears.
We spoke during
that fevered night.
The strains.
Sinews for all to see.

You closed the door.
Threw away the key.

SECTION THREE

He's awake as those sirens raced.
Towards another suffocating place.

Hunger at the Sun Dial

He was never satisfied
with the inglorious
state of play.
As those two
sides unlocked
another pointless display.

He was never satisfied
with any outcome.
The rage all locked out.
Uncovered.
In the past a sober disguise.

The hunger never stopped
though he was still satiated.
In that lane.
The mottled dark.
A sundial so bleakly stark.

Swimming in that
molten stew.
Unleashed his
craven views.
As mysterious
forms floated by.
Drinking in their
ridiculous ruse.

When the
sickening things
took away our
safest things.

The river was never
the nicest thing.

As your smile became
the purest thing.

An Uncertain Wish

Holding my hand
in a certain way.
I never wished it
any other way.
Pulled punches.
Sucked in seasons.
A future embedded
for simple reasons.

But moments played out
like scattered fireflies.
We danced.
Messed about.
Pivots before
their burning eyes.

Listening to those rages
flying by in reams.
I never bothered
to look around.
Keen to keep things
always clean.

A judgement call to Bone.
Always unhelpful
at any time.
Never understood
those car parks.
Or the nonsense
bits in between.

Spitting boldness
from your mouth.
A simple man lost
in his habits.
Cherry-picking your
myriad fantasies.
From a whirlpool
of car crashes.

Walked with you on
lanes and streets.
Ran through mayhem
in parking lots.
Carried endless guilt
into cafes and shops.
Gulped rancid chemicals
in anodyne bars.

Did you ever
know my future.
Such an idea
never felt right.
I knew as high
fives nosedived.
Our heroes kissed us.
Waving goodbye.

Simple things
were never simple.
Those deluded few
who grabbed us.
Spiraling out
into the dark light.

Tethered images.
Our shattered stardust.

All the shouting.
Those unfolding arms.
Watched the cascading
burning litter.
Touched us before
feeling reborn.
Hearing the same
thing sometime later.

Breathing those
cruel hateful ideas.
Thumped me throughout
that night.
Myriad of dirt clumps.
Such fertile lumps.
Tormented in clay.
Your sadistic bite.

A family distracted from
the bleeding news.
Protected those
intractable views.
Friends took an
obvious high jump.
Swerved in sequence.
Unlocked vital clues.

Kissing scorched
uniforms in the circus.
An event witnessed

by all of us.
Double jointed.
Cradling mordant stuff.
Who breathed again
for that uncertain wish.

Blind Hope

Twisting sinking.
A pearl in vain.
Noticing a purpose.
Who carried the flame.
Distant dreams.
We were all afloat.
Simple.
No choice.
He couldn't cope.

Bittersweet.
The taste so cold.
Sweating.
Running.
Seeking your gold.
No head.
Whose head.
A cunning belief.
Tightrope.
Blind hope.
No retreat.

You shared the
same sad dreams.
Forlorn emptiness.
So definitely lost.
Scrambling in blind comfort
to a place no one forgot.

Complete scheming.
Always dealing.

Just done.
No fun.
The vital one.
Can't cope.
A regular scream.
Such fun.
So gone in our new town.

Halos shone.
Those neon skies.
Wishes against potent minds.
Didn't think twice.
Or think again.
To stay safe was
his only domain.

When Angels Flew

It was difficult picking up the pieces.
So much time.
Too many intricacies.

Shadows on walls.
Tiptoeing in apprehension.
Cobbled together half-truths.
Lost in translation.

Tumbleweed silently
kissed the ground.
You kissed a light.
That suddenly burned all around.

It wasn't that I thought or doubted.
As I looked.
Your face so disjointed.

Venturing to go nowhere.
I opened the door.
Sensing an ending.
We'd spoken before.

Scenario.
An image.
A moment so bespoke.
Events.
Sequences.
The inevitable footnote.

It wasn't meant to unravel as it did.
The place we'd stayed.
A place where we couldn't.

Overtures.
Such wonders.
Vitriolic thunder
catapulted everything.
Our roaring rollercoaster.

As if angels were circling above.
I sank.
Replaying significant stuff.

Coruscating stares.
Spittle.
Raging taunts.
Closed my eyes.
Surrendered my tender reward.

Sleeping Horses

Same time.
Lost time.
The boys aren't
up to much.
But look around.
The town's uneasy.
Unhinged.
Old bodies dying
inside designer jeans.

In Manor Royal
outside factory gates.
Spiraling aboard God's
merry facade.
Keeping all the
low life firmly in place.

Bicycles and cars
moved in vain.
Realising everything
once held.
Was never within
anywhere
calm or sane.

Where did we
ever go.
What did we
ever know.
Where did we
ever breathe.

Why did we
never leave.

When on
the horizon
lightening turned
into sea mist.

As our world
remained lost.

No tangible
compass.

Until...

...Charlwood's fields
beckoned with
open arms.
Strolling.
Running.
With the wind
blowing hard.
Watching those
sleeping horses.
Taking everything in
their tranquil stride.

When were we
ever so strong.

Where did we
always belong.

As gravity pulled
our heartbeats together.

Moments
spinning beauty
like no other.

The Thrill of Breathing

The comfort of those four walls.
Clarity.
The only reward.
Bouncing answers
challenged my thoughts.
A perfect moment to calmly smile.

A blank canvas.
Our nerves on heat.
The thrill of breathing.
Punctured stolen hearts.
Never relaxed.
Or unleashed a false start.
Innocence returned.
As fortunes fell apart.

Forgiveness was
never a given.
Platitudes remained
solidly uneven.
We gave way
to heartfelt solitude.
Against spite.
Those glorious few outside.

We were frozen amidst their lies.
Trysts became a different prize.
In the cold.
Wrapped in warm saliva.
No easing back.
No burning other.

As the clowns sipped their tears.
We all stood back.
Paused for nothing.
As the guilt took time to begin.
Anecdotes milked in
caked saccharine.

In the sanctuary of
well-wishers.
We tipped our hats to
famed soothsayers.
Made up.
Pen tied.
Wet withered.
Fulfilment stands in the rain.

A Sense of Timing

He's awake as those sirens raced.
Towards another suffocating place.

Defiance unlocked in shameless flight.
An exacting paranoia so firmly set.

The sense of timing was insecure.
A stuttered joy.
So painfully unfurled.

As fire raged against his blinding sight.
Memories folded into fractured light.

Hanging on to tenterhooks.
He sweated the days away.

Eyes drunk in calm mercy
silenced any false escapades.

We thought he saw things differently.
Running around those dark alleyways.
Singing about the never-never days.

Distant light cloaked his doomed forays
into shadows played in naive times.

Trying to save up all the best lines
for alignments within blind attitudes.

Forsaking every conjured up gratitude.
While running crazy with a grimace in a smile.

Always welcomed by the fierce crowd.
But the desire to try and run again
was never the better option.

Every breath detained.
As fanfares sang to a leaden score.

We watched the moment from a distant shore.
Steps in time were no measured things.

His scream was everything we knew.

And more.

In Wonder

In a mirror.
The image stayed the same.
An anodyne figment.
Untold refrain.
The face a picture.
Composed disdain.
Who'd have thought
you would ever remain.

I wasn't wrong thinking you said.
A necessary boundary.
But everything still bled.
As calmer moments
impressed no one.
Fallen egos collapsed
in languid gloom.

Was I measured
in that furnace.
Striding through
those keen flames.
Cultivating nuanced
melting desires
from distant memories.

Now expired.

A helter-skelter.
I went everywhere for you.
In wonder.
A love laid

out before you.
My heart beating
drums around you.
No lesser path have
I ever pathed for you.

Was I aching
in your crimson rush.
Seeking answers
inside a sunrise crush.

A sliding moment here.
Maybe there.
Your richness
was never so clear.

Such Sweet Gifts

I was never undermined
by your piety.
Or compromised
by your vanity.

It was normal behaviour.
'Sweet' gifts wrapped
up in brevity.

Running in streams
beyond roundabouts.
Encountering many
unnatural habitats.

Your intrinsic charm.
Flame-proofed antidote
to all the sundry fabled slopes.

Who wasn't keen to
mix those thrills.
When sanctuary
stood in tepid spills.

The purpose of taking those perils.
Never entered our heads.
Embittered heroes
in open fields.
We stayed in place.
Upheld routines
to wash our faces.

A deep swim.
A climb high above.
Such punctured joys
never misplaced.

The gift of remembering.
Jolted my heart.
Distant menace embellished
from the start.

The foibles of
bewildering confidants.
Those lukewarm smiles.
Our doomed inheritance.

Was it Ever Enough

You were walking on quicksand.
Missing side hooks
from a firm hand.

Sinking pipe dreams in steam drains.
Skipping ahead to another land.
Cussed memories from the cruel man.

But the ragged toes knew no foes.
Choice mimics in a fake card game.

I was playing with the wind
when you suddenly crawled in.

I couldn't rearrange any moments.
Or quick start a future in time.
As the sense of history
passed me by without a sigh.

When Dust Settles

Peering through the wind in the rain.
Didn't offer anything of the same.

The wet vista.
A mordant terrain.
That cold smirk of an open drain.

Looking up I saw you
on that hill.
Wearing *his* crown.

Arms waving.
Mouth smiling.
Who wouldn't think the same.

But weren't you forgotten
when the dust settled.

A narrowing glimpse
lost in another battle.

You couldn't swing it.
Wing it or
float on the tide.

As all the same
fingers pointed at
your weary demise.

SECTION FOUR

In the playground
I held your gaze.
The mirrored look.
An August haze.

Off

In the playground
I held your gaze.
The mirrored look.
An August haze.

So you're going now.
On your way.

Yes I'm going.
Off on my way.

But what about
our time running.
Chasing.
Climbing our trees.
Looking up at bats.
Screaming
into lanes.
Sliding on
dock leaves.

Why now.
Why are you off.
Seeking.
Troubling.
Gliding on knees.
The river.
Sewer.
Our dams.
What am I
going to do now.

How am I
going to behave.

Where are
you going.
When will
we talk.

This isn't stuff
I know about.
Like the
pavement.
The chalk.
Where am I
going to go.
How will I get
lost on my own.

Why leave
Chelmsford.
It's been our home.
Our orchard.

And I thought
you liked me.
I thought we
were true.
Your house
and gate
are now
closed.

Just like
me and you.

Longing

Things seen
didn't mean
we always played
silly games.
Between the
many dark schemes
we imbued cute
warm scenes.

Knowing when
you stretched.
Looking.
Straining your neck.
Things weren't
all that bad.
Or so we
all thought.

In those cruel
dark days.
You kept me
going in song.
Believing we
could kill time.
Spiralling us all
the way down.

Shadows from
the past.
As hunger duly
kept apace.

Their glance never
meant a thing.
In that bitter
cold place.

You knew when
you held me.
Things could capsize
on the ice lake.
But walking home
always felt right.
Everything conquered
in soaring majesty.

Everything is Never

She was looking
from a distance.
At a memory
held in sequence.

A special shore
in light's crispness.
Turtle tops in
a tundra whiplash.

It was never
clear or forsaken.
If they'd met
the ghost or hadn't.

Simple tricks kept
their simple tasks.
They never knew.
Were never asked.

Same time to
think again.
A reason to try
and understand.

Days forgotten
were never given.
The rush for a wish.
To kiss her haven.

Speeding through
those known streets.
Spiralling towards
their secret treats.

Turning as the
madness uncoiled.
Cold mercies ripped
in muscled thrills.

The mighty crescendo
of blind egos.
Bouncing off those
dark windows.

She could never
let me go.
As we ran headlong
to our sacred hills.

Carried Wisdom

We weren't lost or forgotten.
Acted out in torrid days.
Engendering troubled endings.
Amid mandatory mind games.

Being by Chub Bend
meant everything to the team.
A sodden walk home.
I couldn't hold back
the sherry gleam.

The sun-dappled patterns.
On windscreens in line.
You're heard from a distance.
Amongst the crowds.
Those lustre felines.

Didn't care.
Didn't even notice.
Didn't even want to decide.
It was a chance game.
A pivot.
Our tarnished plan.

Who jumped ship in limbo.
Between a hard rock and a chasm.
The random shock slowly caught us up.
As no one carried any wisdom.

Shifting

Who wasn't nervous witnessing
your dizzying decline.
Head height.
Flailing above the skyline.
A come down so limitless.
All effortlessly benign.
Obscured in blossom.
The wind felt its own taste.

Why did time catch us up
like lose threads.
When it kept
everyone else in its place.
Who knew what doors
were locked or
which ones to push.
Far beyond anyone's sacrifice.

Your calling card never
formed any real answers.
Trust in proper outcomes only
tipped lasting favours.

Thinking was never
your option.
Just as teardrops only
captured ephemeral moments.

Stuff stolen from
every memory.
And shorthand never
evoked anything much.

I never pulled
the clouds
over your eyes.

You were lost
on that faraway coast.

Terrified as the dogs
came pounding through
every hedge row
and uneven pavements.

Never knowing which
gate was safe.

Or which one
was dangerous.

The Slowness of Time

Running across the carriageway.
Crossed our hearts
for another day.
A silhouette
darting in gloom.
Another friend destined
for the higher room.

Clarity of listening
was never heard.
You threw back
those lessons learnt.
Punctured thoughts.
Easy to hide.
Shattered moments in
your fragile world.

Thinking back.
Thinking long.
Hidden stuff was
always wrong.
Never knew or
pathed the way.
For hints of pain.
Your lost forays.

Never easy to understand
what made sense
all the time.

Attitudes.
Those hopeless denials.
A soaring kite hits
that wall tonight.

Never pushed the
button for fun.
The slowness of time.
Judgements all wrong.
As sad faces.
Those streaming eyes.
No cosy
denouements
for the world
you despised.

Holding Fire

Waking up was
easy you said.
The right things
in the right bed.
Subtle nudge.
Those who looked ahead.
A convenient grin.
The starry-eyed who did.

In a moment it
took two shakes.
Slow motion took
time to show.
The ones you
wanted to let go.
Were the ones with
too much to know.

It wasn't always this messy.
Looking from
the marbled periphery.
Your breath nearly
catching fire.
Almost torched
every vivid memory.

Returning home
in a dark dream.
Remember the slip.
A tragic refrain.
Lying alone

in the relentless rain.
Was never the
way to understand.

Thinking again
how you disappeared.
Light smothering
a broken window.
So much serenading.
So many delusions.
Your fetching eye.
The piercing illusion.

Rushing

He wants things to happen.
He wants things to move.

He doesn't care
about provenance.
He's got to get
to that queue.

Gotta go now.
Gotta go hard.
You can't meet
him half-way.

He's soaring high.
Hanging low.
He's a pacemaker
in life's heart.

He's up for anything.
He's up for the whole lot.

Look at him.
He's bleeding.
Seeing everything
he's got.

He's craving.
He's rushing.
He sees the
lake at the top.

Don't push him
or hold him.
He's a light year.
He can't stop.

He's flying now.
So strong.
High above
the vapour trail.
Below the fields
are on fire.
Satiated.
He's found
his Holy Grail.

Asleep in Heaven

Alone in front of fear.
You stood before
the metal steer.

Ghost white amplified
in the sun.
Black shape held
at your side.

From a distance
you looked benign.
A solitary figure
embossed in time.

As it slowly
crawled towards you.
You remained stolid.
So calm.

As the smoke
circled around.
Cries of anger
being shot down.

You were taut.
So very firm.
The moral statue.
A world confirms.
Control was
their anchor.
In silence and
the ether.

It protected their
one agenda.
An agony that
ignites the anger.

Who remembers you
when we all fall asleep.

Who remembers you
when we all fall asleep.

In Fog

The pleasure of smiling
was never a disguise.

Simple things meant
everything for those
who wanted to survive.

On ledges as
sea breezes blew.
Euphoric nights for
the chosen few.

Little heads anointed.
So anew.
As teardrops
flowed into view.

That odd restless moment
when words
mimicked dialogue.

No sense of
any purpose.
Forever lost in
abandoned fog.

Remember that
urgent moment
when the crowd
turned inside out.

Boys finding
their last breath.
Recognising their
sad loss.

The cliché was
their heresy.
Never meant to
be that way.

The two of us
only ever wanted
was a clear day
to simply disappear.

Some Troubled Mind

He burned within
a vividness in time.
Whispered past moments
in entangled rhyme.

Reached out.
Touched me.
He might
have been here.

Looked up.
Looked down.
He was between tears.

Swimming under darkness.
Raging against
the time.

He evoked madness
in a blind nightmare.

Spewing out his
sister's memory.
He sank beneath
the bars.

Losing all his attitude.
Who was that
ever really for.

In vibrant
fairgrounds
alongside such
tight smiles.

A correction was so near
for some troubled mind.

SECTION FIVE

You were lying within a thought away.

Lov (sic)

By shore's resistance I
recounted every given clue.
A mid-life crisis.
Every emerging painful hue.

Was there any elegance about
your initial entrance.
Did people turn and consume
your every sequence.

I remember hearing
only cupped sighs.
No umbrage taken but still
so fiercely despised.

Made in Heaven was never
your place to be.
Pacing the seafront.
Avoiding the bitter sea.

All embracing.
The scene to behold.
Was there ever a better time
to sit back and evolve.
I thought time
would force me
to realise you
weren't mine.
The forgotten one.
My soul hymn.
An installation of
velvet mirth and gin.

But breathing in
that different smile.
Suddenly carried
a new spring
on top of
your precious cloud.

Gone

Cherishing kindness was
never like sunlight.
Such thinking was for
another joyous night.
When the atmosphere
crystalised out of nothing.

I wasn't concerned when
you stood there.
A slight figure smothered
in fake lather.
Windows opened as
gasps deafened every feeling.
Looking at the stars.
A no-exit sign from bedlam.

Choosing whenever
was never a given.
When you spiked my
life in liquid mouthfuls.
History walked on
by as languid no-shows.

I was never the
flower on your balcony.
More a tortured fox
left in a dank burrow.

Melt

I hadn't thought about us.
When issues spilt into view.
Such a simple task I know.
Options to try and think what's right.

Your curled lip spoke volumes.
As tired minds tried to reconnect.
Drifting away from tired playgrounds.
Immersed in our fatal calumny.

I was never that kind of guy.
Though I craved a certain style.
Intuition was never my solid gift.
Significant elements just melted away.

The raw smell of hope.
Never coped with your constant lies.

Everything I'd ever wanted.
Were smoke screens across a wretched sky.

There was never a go-to plan.
No deal to keep things so clear.
The moment you held any meaning.
Was the moment you simply disappeared.

Sometimes Forgotten

The bedroom unfurled
its favourite dream.
No shallow
impulses beyond
anything that screamed.

You were lying
within a thought away.
The cool stream.
Many nights slipping
away from our
chosen scene.

Feeling frozen.
Things blowing anew.
Never knowing when
light came into view.
A sinking feeling
coalesced for
certain times.

Was I floating or
falling in line.

The pure sense of passion
invited my imagination.

Typical travails
through warm fields.

Never an understanding
of things we would see.

*(Confronting those aching
memories meant
everything to me).*

Pure insight.
The revelation it
was always meant to be.

But I was never sure whether
you were your mother's eye.

(That scintillating arc).

As a sunset endorsed
another monumental sigh.

Love Glimpsed

The water tasted different that day.
Punctured with looks so far away.

It was never easy making hay.
When your shadow smothered
every intimate sound.

That photo poured out
those raw emotions.
So drenched.
Every last breath.

An exultant revelation.

I'll never know like I
never knew you.

(*You were the itch
that I never knew*).

I'll never know whether
you ever understood.

(*You were the itch
that never let me go*).

Nowhere Soon

The air smelt of burnt toast
as lilacs danced
against the wind.
Correcting my sight
I saw everything in remote.
Looking again
I realised everything again.

I wasn't scared
when your teeth
bit down hard.
Knowing a fork
in the road
had already torn
us apart.

I knew the night
was nowhere soon.
Life freewheeled outside
in a sharpened curve.

Light was never easy
when I saw what I knew.

Rolling back the tears
I held your gaze for
a final time.
You'd formed
a narrative
that answered
all my fears.

On top of the fountain
above all those
feigning sycophants.
Looks marinated
in fierce egos
thrashing endlessly around.

A borrowed symphony
muted their afterglows.
Carefree after tones
from chosen no-shows.

Drawing a line
in the red sand.

I blew a kiss into
the comforting wind.

Sleepwalking through a Dream

Slow deftness through the night.
Into a forest covered in mist.
I walked alone.
Feelings tempered
as the stars smiled in jest.
Keen affections
laid out on the ground.
Your mouth all around
me laughing out loud.

In a river watching some fish.
Silent mischief within their splash.
As the moon smiled above.
A crystal ball bearing in itself.
The cherished gift
I needed and nourished.

By a roadside I
knelt and glowed.
Shook-up dogs growled
before diving into a canal.
Seconds disappeared.
My locked tongue loosened.
Stemming the flow.

People walked in
discomfort through things
I never knew.
The slow clip clop of their
marching feet.
Sorting out the

ones I believed
I'd never meet.

Here they come now
wanting to take me back.

Everything I remembered
was laid out
and complete.
As the wind
pulled me in I saw
your torn picture
on the concrete.

That smile still
so captivating.
Eyes that melted
the moon's ice.
Now a scattered
image softly
blowing into nothing.

Screaming the Walls Down

Her sweet tear was
something to hold.
A damp rapture
between opening times.
The mirrored vision
in fake marigolds.
Turned in her shadow.
Those blazing eyes.

Killing time never
felt so fine.
Fitness prevailed
in real time.
As sundowners.
Night scowlers.
Pitched up a team
for another crime.

But sanctioning
swimming time.
Never felt comfortable
or divine.
The anxiety
somehow felt fine.
Mustered up falsehoods.
Hallowed charms.

Was she breathing
when I held mine.
Were my eyes closed
when she stepped back.

Did I move.
Kept my lips pressed
when I touched base.
The higher place.

Sunset.

Rag bags threw
nails as happy tags.
As words span
like merry clowns.
Her keeper took
long deep breaths.

Before screaming
the walls down.

Not Now

It was fascinating
how you always caught
the right wave.
But never knew how
to navigate its rightful way.

A blind presence ricocheting
around our new town.
You became emblematic
of an aura serenading 'not now'.

Wishing it had been
a searing dream.
Like a crestfallen angel
circling in time.
Your brother immersed
in that silken slime.

Before sunlight mimicked
every stolen rhyme.
I turned in essence knowing
this was our final 'goodbye'.

Standing alone by
the derelict fairground.
A solitary figure
in relentless decline.

Blinking in the Dark

Forgetting the nuisance was easy.
Second-guessing everything around.
An entity springing up on high fives.
Melting pots of broken young lives.

The bathroom was
different that night.
Thoughts bounced
around this way and that.
A mirror.
An image like no other.
Circled in real time.
You were my saviour.

Gripping the past.
So hesitant.
Turned on memories.
Still relevant.
It wasn't make-believe or cant.
Just signs.
Visions admired as wisdom.

Thirsting for recognition
I scorched the earth.
Sycophants forced
everything into view.
The nonsense.
Those sickening untruths.
Paraded without
needing obvious clues.

A buzzing.
That sense of something.
The noise remained in our heads.
Contradictions exposed
like wet cement.
Urging positive thoughts.
Always stone-dead.

Did we ever get the
things we wanted.
Did we ever get the
things that left their mark.
Did we ever feel energised.
Contented.
Or were we just
blinking in the dark.

In Time

Arriving in time
was the perfect scenario.
Balancing the find.
Nervously looking behind.
Believing anything in kind.

I never knew how
to pace myself.
Things always seemed
to unravel.
I never had a clue
in that certain shadow.

Always lit up.
Distant avenues
never put us
on the straight
and narrow.

Times forsaken.
Blue nights drunk to oblivion.

I was never convinced.
Or ever inclined.
To reconsider who might have
spiked my life.
Or who held the torch
for me in time.

Cold Saw

I kept every memory in a sad pit.
Buried handcuffs in its shallow depths.
Knowing no wisdom or understanding
would form an entity for a certain craving.

Misery was an avalanche of faith.
Careful fallouts turned into fake outs.
Necessary put-downs.
Pure heists.
As the sun turned its heat
onto every conceivable twist.

Squeezing tears for a certain purpose.
I tasted the wind in all its glory.
Secluding a vision.
Realigned into another surface.

From your lips an anxious message
pulled everything away.
No turning heads or queue forming.
No unnecessary kerb crawling
levitated early impressions.

What we heard and what we saw
crushed every agile memory.

All gone beneath the thaw.

SECTION SIX

In the mouths of wolves.
He searched for other fools.

A Kind of Choice

The truest visions always
imposed themselves.
As I sank back into
history's stratosphere.
Uttering words that
were never always clear.
Thinking this will never
be as good as it dares.

A cool breeze opened my
eyes to where I had been.
Remembering the past
was a difficult choice.
Overlapping each
expectation.
I turned as
shadows didn't
know me from Adam.

Wasn't it illuminating that
the choices you'd made
were the ones that
made you afraid.
Nothing circumspect
or indirect.
Just indulgencies from
another bygone age.

Feeling pain is part of
everything we believed in.
Energy suffocating chances

that might have changed.
Looking behind
we never saw
anything to reconsider.
Lost refrains buried
in so many
childhood cadavers.

Did we ever have
time to think again.

Did we ever think
again about our time.

Knowing When

I never mentioned those
moments when I strayed.
So many hourglass
nights openly displayed.
Angel boys running fast.
So far away.
Whirlpools of excitement
crying down every drain.

Those distinct panthers
strutting their stuff
through the rain.
You guessed
what they knew.
And what they might do.
Playing dumb was always
easy when
you never know.
Such a discipline
blowing out like
tepid morning dew.

It wasn't quiet when
you woke up in the sun.
Never seeing the light.
Forever shining on anyone.
All those sleepless nights.
So much of a routine.
When everything else
seemed to be so undone.

Remember us now
as you're curled
up in a ball
beyond recognition.
A presence that
will always be
what you never
wanted to become.

Bland smiles turning
into nights where
darkness has
nowhere left to run.

By Hurricanes

Conjecture after calm tempers.
No time for simple answers.
Meltdowns meant everything.
Vibrant wanderlusts in night flames.

The pointed finger.
A keen backlash
onto a mirrored slapdash.
Turned platitudes into sweet honey.
As hurricanes blew effortlessly by.

In the mouths of wolves
He searched for other fools.
Their smiles held nothing.
Cold tears pulsed inside a rhythm.

There was never any change.
Force-fed.
Vivid contradictions
in the eyes of contretemps.
Tongues licking stained parchments.

In the comfort of idiots.
Dancing through brutal tasks.
Crombie shadows striding across the park.
Grinning to fulfil their majestic pasts.

Something for Tomorrow

My top hat was
a sea change.
Make-up earmarked
a new game.
Didn't clock
those turning heads.
Iconically lost in
our threads.

In dark Wine Alley
we're a stirring crowd.
Glance off each other.
Malice leers down.

Silvi's bottled cute by
the brick-walled fence.
Our desires excited
their fierce stares.

A chip packet
Dave kicks flying.
Hits an Escort windscreen.
Six-foot giants sprawl out
and I'm in the frame.
Searing eyes to
the painted lady.

But a crazed punch from
behind meant for me.
Effortlessly timed.
Strikes his mate.

Who lights out.
Stunned reprieve
for our teen-young brigade.

A better person
was looking on.
He never made
it past page one.

You and I we'd dream
those words clear.
To shut down our
half-naked fears.

I never claimed
any mortal coils.
Or lived hard through
those glorious thrills.
Gliding along Crawley's
lambent hills.
A new-town beckoned
us through.

Old Mirrors

Slowly meeting our needs
we sank gently
to our knees.
Textures caught
us in between.
Captured moments
never before seen.

Warm light.
Crimson silken joys.
Scattered.
Eclipsing everything around.
Who evaporated within
imaginary clouds.
Old habits rooted in
cherished merry-go-rounds.

Why didn't everything
fall into shape.
When did the listening
fail to relate.

You told me I was
worth the wait.
Was I thinking or
simply being polite
when embracing
something called
fate.

Shielding memories from
everything I loved.
Flickering doubts against
guarded nuances.
Feeling out hearts that
never sought assurances.
As condolences flickered
but never shone.

When we looked at each other
were we *really* looking
at each other.

Or were we blinking
into old mirrors.

Images reimposed for
whoever's satisfaction.

A brutal odyssey ripped
apart in open realisation.

Treading Carefully

Remember her
poise that evening.
Ethereal.
Delicate.
In-between light's depth.
It wasn't the stance
that drew our attention.
The shock of her
imminent drowning.
An event sinking
below ominous intentions.

Lending me your voice
made me reconsider
reasons behind every outlier.
You were at last clean.
Virtually buzzing for fun.
Why would you want
to be like anyone.

Comfort joys gone within
the blink of an eye.
Certain attitudes were
never going to decide.
Who agreed to climb
or eventually slide.
Darkness enveloped
her every stride.
Why did I ever want
her to reconsider.
As she unfolded in flames.
Discovering nothing forever.

I wasn't trying to
eliminate her reality.
I was treading carefully.
Skirting quicksand
hidden before me.

Shadow Seen

Didn't you read the ink
or suck in the allegory.

Considered the denouement
but misfired the foreplay.

You meant everything to no one.
And nothing to everyone.

Conjuring low life
 like high fives.
Waxing lyrical.
Akin some shoe shine.

Didn't look innocent
or hamstrung.
Didn't cover dark eyes.
There were none.

You dealt your card.
Flew high.
Good luck.
You ripped up show fly.

There was a level
to your attitude.
No kindred spirit.
Nowhere to go.
Spilt milk never
meant anything.
Just a faultless smile.
Another whim.

In a snake pit to sleep in.
While others left years ago.
I then saw you on
that sodden street.
A distant shadow
with nowhere to go.

safe

Sunlight always smiled
when the wind calmly walked in.
I stroked the pond.
It never turned
as flowers yawned.
Idiots bent down choosing bits
that didn't mean a thing.

Explosions replaced words said.
Meaningful shadows stared.
Gasps in silence
groped around for anyone still here.
Calm soon kissed the atmosphere.
Tilted witnesses charmed everywhere.

Unfolding anything invoked images.
Edges I once balanced on.
In the days when I burned.

My mighty refrain
at last in tune.

I thought light had lost me.
I was wrong.

I'm safe now.
Marinating in a kinder place.

A Certain Fury

The coterie of monsters
flapping by your shoulders.
Swaying from side to side.

We loathed the soft
sound of your hissing.
As you drifted calmly in
and out of our lives.

Looking in sequence
as your ego floated by.

Did we keep
the lights on
when your
world fell apart.

Did the splendour of
your image confiscate
any recognition.

Everything which
balanced our lives
with yours.
Was a caricature of
fortunes from
another world
to savour.

We saw it was
you running
through the sun.

Head tilted back
biting on your
loose tongue.
Was it an
advantage knowing
we weren't
the ones.
From a false
start we were
never in front.

I didn't paint a
rainbow just to
lean you in.
Or smooth over
edges that tightened
any heresy.

Wasn't it funny when
the things you thought
were so threatening
never ventured
outside their box.

You told us everything
would be so right.

Heartbeats
backtracking in
frozen nights.

The way you
wore that crown
evinced a certain fury.

As the crowd
disappeared concussed
by their naivety.

Remembering Snow

Was I looking at you
when you left.
Did I take on
board everything
you said.

Did you need
to be away
to understand
your precious head.

What was all that about.
Then you just
smiled and went.

Does a friend ever
come back to
start all over again.

Do I change anything
if you did.
Does that make
any sense.

Was it all so exhausting.
Melding make-believe
with songs of
joyous wonder.
The intensity of
everything I wanted.
Resonated in the
way you departed.

A distant wave.
The critical horizon.
Wasted footprints
sunk in the ground.

You chaperoned
so many routines.
But *passed* on all
the critical themes.
The looks on our
faces were a picture
for every summer.

Remember.

In dreamscape at night.
Viewing the world
from a scorched map.

Laughing at the
Marx Brothers.
Strong tears
rolling down.

Remember.

Cocking an ear for
a searing moment
to carry us
all back home.

Suddenly everything
was blurred.
An image once

so beautifully formed.
Time slipped
effortlessly by in
correspondence.
A flame that blew.

I'm suddenly in
the arrival lounge.
Pulses to a
maddening range.

I remember.

You're standing there.
Is it really you.
The smile seemed vague.
Your hand was listless.
I wanted to tell you.

I couldn't.

(*About your girlfriend*).

I wanted to scream into you.

I couldn't.

(*Your ridiculous dumb antics*).

I wanted to scratch
into your face.

I couldn't.

(*The drugs are done. All gone*).

The airport became
a seething tinderbox
which burnt the
last light out of me.

And I'm gone.

Remember.

Being with you
was once like
walking on the sea.
A constant meandering.
The sinking.
The ebbs and flows.
I never got caught up
in your history
or afterglows.
Or breathed in
every nuance
from any
unforgotten clues.

In the eye of the storm
I needed something
tangible to bite on to.

I desperately tried
to invoke anything
about you.

A vivid memory
to thrill my mind.
But nothing came
bursting into view.
To embrace my
thoughts around.
Nothing beautiful or intense.
Like when I'm
remembering snow.

Remembering snow.

SECTION SEVEN

A lion's breath under street lights.

Langley Green

Such chatter clatter at the shops.
All held together by the young strops.
A lion's breath under street lights.
Energy gripped in their innate might.

On seats where others sat.
Others stood and calmly spat.
A vivid testament to becalmed youth.
Teen icons awaiting their final cough.

On rooftops keenly displayed.
The mighty stood.
 A charmed parade.
Screaming virtues of their crusade.
Eyes of wonder at their fingertips.
Heaven built on spools of Betamax.

By an oak tree.
Spinning yarns agog.
Crowds hung onto every aspiring snog.
Aching indulgences.
The parents are so remote.
Crystalised strengths.
While shadows never spoke.

In Larkspur

Young heads swerved
out of the gloom.
An open door
presented ideal rooms.
Shining tiles below
glittering lights.
Stunned nourishment
in rich delights.

Bouncing off the
whims of bright things.
The dance floor pirouetted.
Eventful joys.
On sidelines we
respectfully smiled.
As Maggie May serenaded
our sated desires.

Footie tables attracted
the usual crowds.
Toilets collected
their panoply of clowns.
Eyes pinched on mirrors.
Imbibing latest wows.
Outside by garages.
Dark figures scowled.

Those nights we
glued onto everything.
Disco.
Bar.

The television room.
Interludes confiscated
potent glooms.
A phoenix rose.
Captured the right hues.

The sparkling temple.
The bleak woods.
Pocketed beating hearts.
Those fresh hoods.
Pathways towards fated adult throats.
Saved.
The ones who always understood.

Near Cherry Lane

On planks and
ladders they swarmed.
Eyeing us up
as timid pawns.
New builds in
stunned turmoil.
Febrile interlopers
for a new town.

Closer.
Their shrieking
doubled down.
Looking at the
stark wilderness.
Making sense
of the situation.
Milk teeth nemeses
smiling in the rain.

Tossed stones.
A scything arrow.
Weapons glistened.
The afternoon throng.
Together walking
toward their kingdom.
The fireflies danced
in chaotic frissons.

In a ditch.
Gleamed their fears.
A gift noticed

through tumbled leaves.
Epiphany.
They shed the same tears.
In mud.
Inhaled potent
smoke dreams.

Images burnt through
my nightmares.
A natural torrent.
Children at play.
Mature now.
Not punctured
or confined.
Adolescents
once broken.

Saved.

At Ifield Shops

Outside the chippy
we serenely sat.
Paul with his butty.
Me with scraps.

Moonbeams illuminated
concrete steps.
In wonder we watched
the night waking up.

A fierce smack.
A sharp sound.
Turning to face
two figures found.

Fallen body.
A force profound.
Black/white motif.
The bloodied pond.

Watching.
Stretching our eyes.
By the playground.
Another divide.

Moments to
redirect our minds.
Standing.
Cold hearts in
broken mouths.

Calmness now.
The fractured night.
Restless souls in
frenzied flight.

Spreadeagled visions
grasped our plight.
Running home to
the comforting light.

The Embassy Cinema

(Outside) a cloudless night sky
pushed shadows into full flight.
Wailing blurs curdled
in waves of steaming teeth.
Pacing the pavement.
Racing towards their
chosen wraiths.

Kicking cans off the kerb side.
A unison.
Angled postures
sequenced in grey.
Open garden gates.
Clowning screeches distended.
The terraced legion
parachuted into
dank garage lots.

Eagle tattoos flying
between mighty blades.
Vivid smiles.
Fervent make believes
from The Floodlight.
As we span into
their fevered view.

Striding ahead.
Blessed with
even pulses anew.
Woven.
Ignited.

We kissed the
scabrous evening '*ciao*'.

Crouching quickly the fist
parted your wispy hair.
Looking behind sensing
the moment we'd feared.
A whiplash.
Rabid torn sequences.

Laughing at our dalliances.
Two boys in full flow.
Running.
Embattled.
Harassed hares snatched
the Wimpy sign we dived.

(Inside) McMurphy scanned
our novel faces.
We glued onto
his every mien.
Manic laughter from
the hospital ward.
Mirrored our stricken
insights into
what we saw.

I never forgot
the ending or
the foreboding music.
It supercharged my life.
A belief in
the human spirit.

Travis sat before us.
In his taxi with Betsy
in the back.
The tortured man.
A history festooned in blood.
We turned in wonder asking
'*was this us*'.

Effigies smothered
on a garlanded rug.
Never knowing our futures.
We burned the bitter lamp.

Hearts wrenched inside
a carapace of light.
Two films locked
in our consciousness.
Which one would
mean the most.

The potent forerunner
for our latent ghosts.

Around Queen's Square

Off the bus we're sprinting
towards the square.
Turning to Dave
we're almost there.
Colin's not far behind
grinning in the sun's glare.
Shoppers everywhere
spinning yarns we
don't bother to hear.

Cloaks around the back.
Door open beckoning me in.
New albums to ruminate on.
Buzzing inside.
A solid track playing
to the throng.
Rifling through the racks
I grab the one I want.

Walking past the fountain.
New town kids in play.
Mums and dads
watching not
far away.
All good fun
but the police keep
a keen eye.

*(Starlings squawk and
scatter into an inviting sky).*

Standing in the taxi kiosk.
The coolest place in
the square.
Always a mystery
as to why it was there.
Never saw a taxi but knew
some were near.
Go-to place for
messy catch-ups.

(*Mordant shadows played out*
in sunlight).

Sunday mid-day.
On the bandstand
the coolest bands play.
We watch and
listen in awe.
Swigging bottles
and smoking whatever
we've scored.
Time danced with us
as the day became
one and soared.

Three hundred yards away
the college stood and swayed.
My first venture into
Adulthood where I
delved and found
my brain.

Breathing deeply my
world started here.
Sparkling.
All the tired gimmicks
had disappeared.
Believing now
I turned and faced the sky.
Joyous bloomed.
I am saved.

One Night in the Johnnie

As the doors
flew open Mr. O'Hara's
voice soared towards
gilded Heavens.
Moon winked.
Star spun.
A theatre filled
with Irish kin.

Paul's stag do raged
in the public bar.
Webby farting in
the gents to his
heart's content.

*'Anyone want any selfish
in here'* her voice
shrilled across the room.

Abuse drowned her out
from those who wished
to fill their boots.

Barred-for-life
locals hid under
crooked tables.
Dark glasses
reflecting ribald glares.
Like a distinct image
curled up inside
the saloon fire.

Bone pitched his lines
to score the night's
glory flames.

Our evening's very
own mercy gift.
It waited in the
beer garden by
the wooden gate.

Lager doused us
into stunted numbness.
Mordant laughter greeted
the final closing bell.

Stumbling out into
a weary darkness.

Happy hours melded
into one night's
amplified excesses.

Chasing Stars

As snow licked our foreheads.
Running towards those chosen barricades.
Living clues biting the wrong throats.
Waving flags displaying other quotes.

Keeping sake was never an easy task.
Splinters cosy for the biggest ask.
No side entrance to bear witness.
Lessons learnt.
The very notice given.

The line of light was moments away.
Simple feelings stretched different ways.
Knowing the joys of borrowed times.
A spirited rush as terror bells chimed.

Those forgotten pipe dreams.
Were never what they seemed.
The courage to swim against the tide.
Was an option for a certain wunderkind.

Looking up we saw the natural prize.
As light began inching through.
Scratching the surface.
A dappled poise.
Who wasn't enthralled with chasing stars.

The Day When Night Arrives

The measured hope.
And gleaming tears.
Set down the markers
for our significant years.

When the time arrived
to spark the gain.
Outcomes were never the same.

In shattered earthquakes.
We never swallowed anything
or took nothing for granted.

(*The Prism borrowed us
some melted time*).

But beyond the day
the moon was so alive
amidst your swamp smile.

As the falling light
caught all the pain.

We turned away
in anguished fright.
As the ghosts fled
with joyous delight.

The ones we lost
in their guided flight
was the almighty cost.

(*From our darkened past*
we saw the crown).

Such a piercing time
sunk in pure velvet shine.

A penny for your thoughts
was never our way.

The tangled nonsense
crept up then sulked away.

Like giants towering above
hillsides and other glades.
Everything tense in adult throats.
All caught up with no let-up.

Those soaring kites.
Once a showtime in another life
were suddenly blown away.

And with the undeniable truth.
That day always gives way
to an unpredictable night.

SECTION EIGHT

As fog slowly covered
your illusive shape.
Smoke rings formed
from your icy breath.

The Tiredness of Sleeping

Underneath your room.
Dream-like movement below.
Moment to dark moment.
I shake and unwind in time.

(*Sunk in memory.*
I suffocate in noise).

Outside in dusk's umbrella.
Stringent sounds blister.
I catch Steve's banter.
As he suddenly adjusts.

Smoke rings
circled in play.
Steve's face
duly mottled.
My house a
byzantine scene.
Complexities
twist inside.
In my room.
Undercover.
Shaft-sunk in sound.
Muted screams in
a dead hope.
My once vivid colours
now bleached.
(*Sunk in memory.*
I suffocate in noise).

In light I
see you're here.
Reach out.
Take me.
A sunlit energy.
Your warm synergy
breathing in.

Unhurried Glories

I was scared when
you let me down.
All secrets.
There to play around.
Everything open.
Everyone to digest.
A private affair.
Unleashed on the rest.

All those unhurried glories.
Either lived in or caressed.
You took the wish
out of wishing.
Outcomes measured
until the last.

Do you remember
the lightning.
Scratching across
that dark sky.
We hid under
those dust sheets.
Immersed.
Nestled in swoon mist.

A desire to run
with the crowd.
Was never
something transpired.
But you carried on rapidly.
The blind spot
embossed in misery.

In the solitude
of awakenings.
You kept the
hints all secret.
Hidden in
triumphs of thinking.
Amid the no-nonsense liaisons.

Picking rare
times in motion
from the other
side of the mountain.
A thing you
screamed out for.
An inch away.
Dormant from
another shore.

Where They Stood

On tops of trees
he saw everything.
Across the sky a
town on its knees.
As were all
those make-believes.
Running around
like rabid banshees.

Vultures tearing at
hearts of the beaten.
A smile.
That smirk.
So driven.
No playful hug.
Or eyeball of passion.
My shed.
A place drenched in poison.

Along the dual carriageway.
This is where they stood.
Fierce giants from
the Crombie age.
Noble hearts buried
in secure neighbourhoods.

In subways we saw
those young boys.
Holding flames like toys.
Sniffing stuff.
Awake with dark memories.

Never held much.
The slow dripping
of a leaking tap.

In winter as
nightmares eerily rose.
A reason to re-engage.
Or self-promote.

Never going to reconcile those.
As snow fell.

Ice took on a different note.

Comparing Light

Did the pillow turn
when I cried.
Or was that
the moment when
you'd arrived.
The hushed image.
Was it mine.

As dark as
night's symphony.
Shadows still
struggled to dance.
Your smell knocked me
sideways on the beach.
Such a yearning
still within reach.

Was I floating in a well.
An effort to
align my ground.
Echoes heard.
Was anybody found.
As light darkened
slow panic entwined.

Handstands adorned
your entrance.
Standing back
I sensed the morning
amid gleams
of elastic wonder.

Descending slowly
to savour definitions
against the sun.
A vision in
isolated splendour.

As fog slowly covered
your illusive shape.
Smoke rings formed
from your icy breath.

Light breathed
in the pain.

Crushed memories of
times lost within
a certain place.

Stilts

When the sky burnt our hearts.
We looked for signs.
Fresh starts.

Underwater never
kept anything apart.
Meeting anyone
would always hurt.

What impact did
we really need.
An attitude to
eventually succeed.

The audience tried
to believe.
Our playground.
A place to retrieve.

Fireworks alive
in my garden.
Many smiles
kindled in unison.

Looking up.
Those startled skies.
All forgiven.
The rehearsed contrition.
By a lake.
The crowd eerily moved.
Moonlit haloed.
Soaked in lies.

Grinning shapes
in sharp demise.
A noble entrance.
Your wasted disguise.

Running down the hill.
Fags in mouths.
Cascading rain
encasing our souls.

Lights of the Johnnie
still within view.
Like standing on stilts.
So much to imbue.

Drinking those
blinding moonbeams.
In telescopic
chaotic daydreams.

Stray heads afloat
in murky slipstreams.
We played catch up
in stunning ravines.

Could things have
been any different.

So many stark
inconsistencies.
Danced around our
craven taste buds.

Were we always force-fed.
Our satiated epiphany.

This (is)

Your movement
on the floor
was a gift to view.

So much blondness
mesmerised the
evening's hue.

There was a moment.
This is it.

Reality screamed
in spellbound fits.

As the herd
punctured on to
tunes hummed in myths.

So much forgotten now.
So much forgotten before.

So much never wanted.
So much withering
on the vine.

A field stolen in time.
Glories span me around.

Never thought I could fly.

Or feel ten feet high.

I'm not turning the tide.

Or delivering on cue.

Just measured calmness
being there for me and you.

Some Glorious Miles

In light at the beginning.
Your shape by the window.

Looking out unburdened.
An image trapped in day glow.

It was never easy or clear
if I was with you or near.

But the moment you turned
was the moment
everything became history.

We're out now avoiding the lies.
Walking tall.
Sketching those skies.

Dripping joy with
effervescent smiles.
Our future beckoned in
some glorious miles.

It was never easy
seeing those waves.
When all the surf
had turned away.

But your silhouette
was always there.
Shimmering towards
my crested chimes.

Hanging in meant
another change of gear.
Looking cool embroiled
so many fears.

But I'm up now
sucking in your atmosphere.
A testament to puncture
thoughts we weren't ever there.

Nothing

Looking at those
sepia photos wasn't
the reason I held back.

There was nothing
left in my feelings
for you to control.

Was I thinking clearly
when you tripped
up before me.

Lightening only strikes
twice you said.
But that third time
tilted our heads.

Pitch perfect.
Never the pitch
we played on.
As silent voices
chimed as one.

Sun-soaked.
As soaked within reason.
No thinking.
No warmth.
Nothing.
It wasn't time
that caught the air.
As forced liaisons
made so clear.

You scattered your
linear collage.
Conjured yourself
the mermaid.

I walked foolishly
in your history.
Hollow steps
lodged in mine.

Being young I
never felt guilty.
Innocence dazzles
in its symmetry.

Watching Swallows

When the night disappeared
you turned in your golden mystery.

Forged all those sun-tinted days.
A tuning fork in our trajectory.

So deep in our
drug-scarred sanctuary
in those teen-dark moments.

Your tough wild kindness
calmed all my tender senses.

Never tasted the wind without you
or span webs between us.

And the concert lights you pointed to
were the ones we always clung to.

In all the Zeppelin
times we shared
before the moment you flew.

I remember when we watched
swallows piercing
into darting view.

Darting across those
tumbling hills.

We looked in joy.
Their soaring wonder.

A new open door.

Another life with me.

Another life with you.

SECTION NINE

Treading on my bones.
You skipped away lightly.

Aplomb

Was the ghost asleep
when we passed it by that night.

I remember the road was empty
and the shop was still shut.

The calm you eschewed
was emblematic of
everything we knew.

Flying high never found space.
As all the looks had the same face.

(*The little things grew up*
to be the bigger things
we all despised).

We were so near.
A sense of being there.

Every icon we witnessed.
Dissected.
Dancing with majestic dignity.

A poignant reminder
of all the times
you crushed nightmares
with alacrity.

But you knew
the real moment

when your star
shone that night.
A stunning image
forever in light.

The Sadness of Knowing

Was it really
the defining moment.
Noticing in the photo
that you weren't present.
You had been elevated.
Seeing something
before tomorrow.
Even though you were
scared of your own shadow.

When the sky portrayed
its beaming colours.
You were blindsided
by those broken mirrors.

Appearing like icy mist
on a silver stream.
Warmly licking everyone
you'd ever seen.
Hang fives.
Sentient hugs.
Smiles beaming.
Behaving like you
were never leaving.

The shock when you
suddenly withdrew.
From The Wreck that night by
those burning bridges.
Mates on the patches
looking out for the bizzies.

Skitting on grass.
Breeding under night's canopies.

It was summertime drunk
as a winter's brew.
Under an anchored moonlight.
Holding its view.

Looking across the park
I saw you quietly turn.
Hands in pockets like
you were walking
towards another land.

A sober image openly displayed.
As the sadness of
knowing nothing will ever
be the same again.

Awake on the Avalanche

Luminescence bloomed
in that yellow dress.
Introducing herself vividly
to an adoring crowd.
Crystal smiles
savoured for all times.
Glances anchored into
every boy's future dream.

On the avalanche thinking
as the clouds waltzed by.
A meandering white flow
pierced the sleepwalking blue.
Who knew when we
would ever know which way.
Thinking back did we
need to know anyway.

(Come on I'll sleep where I can.
I'm beside myself.
I can't look where I've been.
A cold closet marooned in shamrock green.
Was it good to answer or so I believed).

I'm lost.
I'm here.
I'm gone.
I'm near.
Where am I.
I thought I was nowhere.
Complete.

So neat.
Look up.
Dissect.
I'm not going
anywhere in this heat.
Breathing in.
So clean.
I'm beyond feeding
into any machine.

The air.
The moon.
No more sun
hurrying up soon.
When were the clouds
going to move and slant.
The river's in a bind
above our notion groove.
Luckless blends were always
wasted on anything that moved.

Setting the Seas on Fire

Part One

I'm running.
Running.
Running.
Above tree tops
in moonlight.

Spinning plates
in lockdown.
Visions in
gleaming snowdrops.

Black cars breezed in.
Shadows piercing headlights.

Old habits never died.
Potent symbols never tried.

On rooftops
and bit shops.
Echoes never
went away.

No shoeshine
or trace line.
Solid eye marks
in chalk lime.
Immersed in
clichéd deadlock.
Built up on
worn hard luck.

Treading on my bones.
You skipped away lightly.

Such a noted valediction
for a once-searing beauty.

Part Two

Inhaling shadows
in distant rooms.
Falling asleep but
still marooned.

A split second
caught in headwinds
as screams
misled the chase.

Clinging onto
something else
my eyes searched
the south coast.

Forever balancing
latent fury
with things I
loved the most.

In the minds of many.
Memories locked
in a frozen maze.

Lost on doomed
motorways.
Confounding those
who didn't care.

I'm folding mountains
into templates.

Transforming twilight
into pure light.

Consuming my
contagious desires.

Knowing everything
was within time.

Before setting
the seas on fire.

Silent Moments

Was something aglow in the dark.
A wrap-around worth top marks.
Seeking out mermaids in swim time.
An event to behold.
To feel fine.

A thing to drip feed in.
Moments they rarely thrived on.
So much glory hunting.
Night screams.
Running fast amidst silent streams.

Mixed messages often crisscrossed.
Snow blinded by his daily loss.
Sad souls still crying out there.
Measured in bright sequined gloss.

There was no time to figure out
when night took hold.
Did we nearly manage.
Was it okay.
Or did time just slowly slip away.

In a Different Lift

The sense of wonder
was never a given.

A last sigh
in your breath
was the sound
of thunder.

In corridors of myths
you flipped those vital yarns.

Special feelings
you once said
were many
vivid charms.

But the places
where we went
were never ever safe.

Looking up I
thought I saw you.
An image from
a different lift.

In a solitude
of likeness
all crammed in
such tightness.

Thinking became timeless.
The outcome hostile.
Numbness.

Did we ever
clear our throats
before we swallowed
or choked.

The ones that never
made a fuss
were the ones
who lost the most.

Chewing on the
fat of heroes
never gave
anyone a chance.

As all the bursting
glitter just fell into
our battered crowns.

Pure Grace

Was there clarity in the imagery
you laid out before me.

I wanted true signs in real forms.
A fire kiss from your heart storm.

Never wanted to dictate.
Never deemed to be in top shape.

Only by notion.
Your natural bloom.
Standing before me in pure grace.

As your warm eyes melted
my friends in every scene.
I saw a sunrise in purple sunbeams.
Earmarking a path to iced diamonds.

I realised it was you I needed
to negate any mad hesitancy.
Easing me down beautifully.
To the pivot of your unerring beauty.

Burnt Sacrifices

In the heartlands
of glorious envy.
I treasured pathways
to your spellbound memory.
Being lost in the
mercies of burnt sacrifices.
I studied a newborn
world to finally survive in.

Peering through waterfalls.
Things neatly fell into place.
Lifelong partnerships
laid out in front of me.
Images never seen
now spinning before my face.
Like walking with an angel
to a glorious destiny.

SECTION TEN

As light lingers.

Catching Rainbows

Wasn't it telling when
you thought you'd made it.
Was the moment we all knew
you'd taken the wrong exit.

And didn't time fly when
we thought you'd reached it.
Spectators looking on.
Sharpened eyes.
As something moved in wilting trees.

And who was catching rainbows
when those changes suddenly arrived.
Memories never left hallowed spaces.
Colours wrapped in indecent haste.

Glistening hopes in fields of tears.
Sharp nonsense kept in close arrears.
You knew everything didn't you.
Illusions sculptured for the noble few.

In Awe

Running towards the
farm was fun.
A farmer behind
clutching his gun.
The police blindly
lost in heather.
No margin for error.
Fit kids.
Never.

At Chub Bend.
A slide to the river
kept the fit kids safe.
Breathing together.
In a lane the farmer
struggled making sense
as the police ran towards
a no-exit fence.

In the water we
heard their voices
cursing our agile
disappearance.
Anger at full throttle.
We waded in sequence.
Muted cygnets.
A drifting radiance.

Such potent blue
meant everything.
Striding through wetness

between chaos.
Never looked behind
or cared for much.
Just stretched out.
Gathered warm moss.

Trenchant times
drifted from the blue.
Pent up.
Such a solid melancholy
as growing up
was never subtle.
Dreams collided
with eclectic days.

Like...

The fit men went by
the farm the other day.
All banged up.
Cobwebbed.
Tooth decayed.
His gun out to
pasture with the cows.
The police station derelict.
A tortured ghost house.

An Impression

Was it the moon that
dealt you that blistered hand.
Witnessing the thunder
obliterating every futile plan.
A checkered history mirrored
in a specious wonderland.
Unforgiving.
An image in pigments
laying stagnant on the sand.

Who was diving into the
perimeter of your dreams.
Colours so washed over in
those technicolour greens.

A Monet gilded in sepia gleams.
No one ever forgets
what they think we ever mean.

Beyond the Curve

You startled my interest.
Played havoc with my intentions.
The territory had looked bleak.
Pastures barren.
Lacklustre intrigue.

Watching your vibrant shadow.
Lean.
Taught.
A rush to meet.
At the end so svelte and petite.
Mesmerising.
So bewilderingly neat.

It wasn't near anything.
A bit thing in a firestorm.
I looked out wearily into the rain.
All the naked chaos.
The petty damned.

I didn't always have to struggle.
Or beg for time off in lieu.
You knew where I was going.
You knew which road I'd choose.

Just in Whispers

A quietness.
So obvious.
Ears pricked against the wind.
Expecting everything to begin.
I didn't want any screaming.
Just whispering.
Heralding a peaceful time.

Quietness.
Deep into the night.
Always kissing.
Jewels in flight.
Just like those whispers.
So intense.
Always enough.
For everything I needed to decipher.
And so much more.
Any abject sounds
freewheeled like thunder.
We lined up which ones weren't vital.
And what ones entangled us in wonder.

Until we knew
which ones to discover.

Forever.

Boys Own

Was it the right time
to shoeshine the wrong guy.
All the leather in
one straight line.
A terrible burden for
such a fragile mind.

You knew those
boys were no good.
Smirks of hyenas.
Never misunderstood.
Wish washed in
their salad haze.
Cruel types never
fully displayed.

On top of
the eternal cusp.
You witnessed
everything too fast.
It wasn't for
any meal ticket.
Moments cushioned
your eternal hit.

In that dripping subway.
A figure drenched.
Your nascent enemy.
Sneering at you.
All overt malice.
Plundered your
precious palace.

Those vile dark days.
No canvas blinking.
Unleashing his vicious ways.

On the south coast
you sought solace.
A protective ring.
Some peace of mind.
Gracious suburbs.
Welcoming.
Fomenting your
perfect desires.
Growing tall amid
the shadows of the blind.

Strength at last in a
loving pair of hands.

Eclipsed

Those beautiful words
you poured over me.
Engendered lucid evenings
in warm nectar.
A nocturne residence
inside a unique ravine.

The bellwether who
compounded my desires.
As waterfalls rainbowed
in luscious colours.
All thinking was done.
Everything felt so alive.
Your smile transfixed
Into a marble image.

Looking up I saw
the full circle unfolding
in stunning candour.
White then black.
A triumph of
inimitable wonder.
We gravitated towards
our gilded future.
Knowing nothing would
ever hold us back.

Akin

I am complete.
Walk in the skies to breathe.
Sleep in nectar with some bees.
Swim in the seas.
With beasts that might harm me.

But I see serpents
and wish them well.

Carrying water to fields that need to grow.
Laughing with creatures that already know.

Wake up and play with the sun.
Balance everything before me.

Collapse with the intangible weight.
The weight.
Before it kills me.

Landfill

Was it the timing or the light.
That left us stranded that night.
Looking out.
The lie of the land.
Vivid moments we forgot to fill.

Was it painful keeping all that stuff.
That carried on holding us up.
Those days would always be there.
Stark images scarring us all for life.

As the reams of paranoia
enriched the chosen few.
The footloose lost their balance.
Ever tumbling out of our view.

Through a vortex of imminent chaos.
Would those secrets soon consume us.
As speeches repeated in pathos.
Will all our beliefs be left in tatters.

We were so warm within the contours
of how we behaved.
Recognising those tears
we knew were
ours to finally save.

Flirting with Wasps

Counting fingers
on one hand.
Never counted when
things got out of hand.

Stirring feelings
of those unkind.
Captured everything
within a closed mind.

Running fast to
mercifully catch up.
Throwaways lingering
near bleak spots.

Never a race
to match that.
Reaching out to who
we met each night.

Stretching out into
no man's land.
Leaned into me.
I needed to
see your plan.

Kept me close
thinking I was lost
in a wasp nest.
The uninvited guest.

Testing everyone
with oblique diatribes.
No nonsense fairy tales.
Listless.
I'm tired.

Filtering this way.
The ersatz brickbats.
On a clear day
singing to wisecracks.

Sucking mannerisms
through leaking straws.
Pinpointed hope in
a furrowed new town.

Carry on laughing
you said.
Just carry on.
No tide turns when
you hit the stop button.

But don't tip me over
now as I might drown.

Stirrings from the Furnace

1

Many fingers balletically point.
Cruel whispers sting like foghorns.
He stands in full view.
The human cotton bud.
Shaking with pain in
his steaming slip-ons.

On a broiling train in the highlands.
Watching glens idle gloriously by.
Sun's rays dazzle and dance.
He's a presence muffled
amongst the crowded noise.

Breath hissing.
Bandaged grey cocoon.
Eyes alert.
Untethered but marooned.
No one to comfort.
Console or prepare.
For a life unwrapped.
An unsparing world.

2

Bursting chaos through the clouds.
Smoke balloons.
Hot metal pieces scatter.
Roars a demise for Skye.
Catastrophe's disguised in
a Hudson bomber.

On the ground the
silver wreckage sighs.
His eyes closed.
Licking red tongues everywhere.
As smoke snakes
through the sky overhead.
A Canadian drags
a young airman clear.

3

Confronting provenance.
He stands by the Meadows.
Where he ran.
Chased.
Under adolescent halos.
Memories constrict.
Grip him like arm locks.
Young Tim.
Fearless.
Adorned in shamrock.

A tenement flat in Edinburgh.
His family sits aghast.

Overcoat formed
in the hallway.

Blue forage cap slanted.
Stunned gasps
pepper the ether.

4

..."my son is a MONSTER"...

...silence hugs my gaping loss.
Tears steam in deep wounds.
As light lingers.
I'm alone in my own furnace.

About Atmosphere Press

Founded in 2015, Atmosphere Press was built on the principles of Honesty, Transparency, Professionalism, Kindness, and Making Your Book Awesome. As an ethical and author-friendly hybrid press, we stay true to that founding mission today.

If you're a reader, enter our giveaway for a free book here:

SCAN TO ENTER
BOOK GIVEAWAY

If you're a writer, submit your manuscript for consideration here:

SCAN TO SUBMIT
MANUSCRIPT

And always feel free to visit Atmosphere Press and our authors online at atmospherepress.com. See you there soon!

About the Author

T C **WALSHE** started writing poetry in early 2021 and lives on the South coast of England, UK.

Printed in Dunstable, United Kingdom

65107860R00129